j796.96
ITA

$13.95

Italia, Bob

HOCKEY LEGENDS

3 9077 03198852 3

CHILI PUBLIC LIBRARY
3235 Chili Avenue
Rochester, NY 14624

OCT 25 '93

Hockey Legends

by Bob Italia

Published by Abdo & Daughters, 6535 Cecilia Circle, Bloomington, Minnesota 55439

Library bound edition distributed by Rockbottom Books, Pentagon Tower, P.O. Box 36036, Minneapolis, Minnesota 55435

Copyright© 1990 by Abdo Consulting Group, Inc., Pentagon Tower, P.O. Box 36036, Minneapolis, Minnesota 55435. International copyrights reserved in all countries. No part of this book may be reproduced in any form without written permission from the publisher. Printed in the United States.

Library of Congress Number: 90-083608   ISBN: 1-56239-009-0

Cover Photo by: Bettmann Archive and Wide World Photos
Inside Photos by: Wide World Photos
          Page 25 Bettmann Newsphotos

Edited by Rosemary Wallner

— Contents —

The crowd—the goal—the exciting game of hockey.

Introduction

Hockey is a complicated sport that requires many athletic skills. A player must have great balance, quickness, and strength. To become a great hockey player, one must have all these qualities— plus the determination to be the best. Throughout their careers, these five hockey players have shown their talents and their determination, and have dominated their sport in the years they have played.

Bobby Orr flies past Chicago Black Hawks goalie
Tony Esposito to score a goal.

Mr. Hockey

Robert (Bobby) Orr was born March 20, 1948, in Parry Sound, Ontario, Canada. His father, Doug, had his son on skates by the time Orr was three years old. Orr skated on a nearby frozen pond. He fell often, but would always get up again, determined to skate. Skating came naturally to Bobby Orr. Soon Orr was skating just as well—and as fast—as boys who were older than him.

In Canada, most boys played hockey. Orr was no exception. Because he could skate so well and so fast, he became a very good hockey player.

When he was fourteen years old, Orr became an All-Star defenseman with the Oshawa Generals, an amateur team. By the time he was sixteen years old, Orr was considered the best high school hockey player in Canada.

Orr had to wait until he was eighteen years old before he could play professional hockey. He signed with the Boston Bruins of the National Hockey League (NHL) in 1966. As a defenseman in his rookie (first) season, Orr scored 13 goals with 28 assists for a total of 41 points. He often got into fights with older opponents who wanted to intimidate the young rookie. But Orr was determined to show everyone he was good enough—and brave enough—to play in the NHL. At the end of the season, Orr was named Rookie of the Year.

During the 1967-68 season, Orr suffered the first of many knee injuries. He played only 46 games, scoring 11 goals with 20 assists. Still, he received the Norris Trophy for being the best defenseman in the NHL. Not only was Orr a great skater who could play outstanding defense, he also had a powerful, 100-mile-per-hour slap shot. He could put the puck in the net like no other defenseman had ever done before.

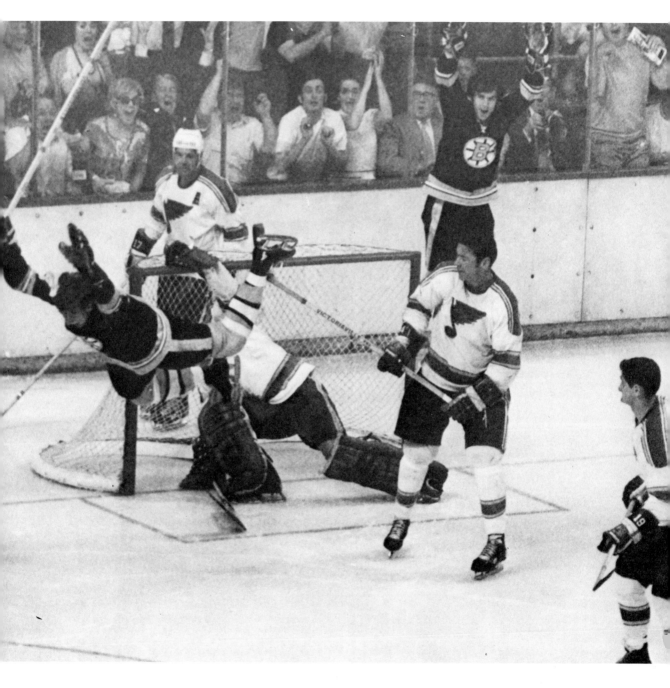

Bobby Orr flying thru the air after scoring a goal—
this all-out effort caused Bobby many injuries.

In the 1968-69 season, Orr scored 21 goals with 43 assists for 64 points, leading the Boston Bruins to the Stanley Cup play-offs. Though the Bruins were beaten in the semifinals, people began to take notice of Boston and Orr. Other teams knew the Bruins would soon become a powerful force in the NHL.

The very next season, Orr had one of his finest years. And so, too, did the Boston Bruins. Orr scored 33 goals and established a league record for assists with 87. His 120 points won him the scoring title. No other defenseman had ever won this title. That year, Orr led Boston into the Stanley Cup play-offs. In 14 games, Orr scored 9 goals with 11 assists. In the final game, Orr scored the winning goal in sudden death. For the first time in twenty-nine years, the Boston Bruins had won the Stanley Cup. Orr was named Most Valuable Player (MVP) in the play-offs and the entire league.

In the 1970-71 season, Orr tallied 37 goals and 102 assists for an amazing 139 points. His 102 assists were an NHL record. For the second year in a row, Orr was named the league's MVP. A year later, Orr led the Bruins to their second

Stanley Cup in three years. For the third straight year, Orr was named MVP of the National Hockey League. Sportswriters everywhere began calling Orr "Mr. Hockey."

In 1972, Orr suffered a serious knee injury that required major surgery. Everyone thought Orr's career was finished. But Orr came back in the second half of the 1972-73 season to score 29 goals with 72 assists. He was awarded the Norris Trophy for the sixth straight time.

Orr suffered more knee injuries in the following years. Each time he had surgery, Orr's skating speed was affected. He missed many games. In 1976, Orr was traded to the Chicago Black Hawks who used Orr's name to draw crowds. But Orr realized he could no longer play the way he once did. He retired at the end of the 1977-78 season.

During his amazing career, Orr, a seven-time All-Star, shattered all scoring records for his position. If he had not been slowed down by injuries, Orr might have become one of the greatest scorers in hockey history.

Espo

Philip (Phil) Esposito was born February 20, 1942, in Sault Sainte Marie, Ontario, Canada. Like most young Canadian boys, Esposito was on skates shortly after he learned to walk. His first skates were double-bladed. The blades were tied with leather straps onto his boots. Esposito learned to skate and play hockey on a small ice rink in the backyard of his home. He often played with his younger brother, Tony. Tony Esposito would one day become a famous goaltender with the Chicago Black Hawks.

Phil Esposito's early years with the Chicago Black Hawks.

When Esposito was ten years old, he tried out for a little league hockey team. He did not make the team. Disappointed, Esposito practiced hard and made the team the following year.

Esposito attended St. Mary's High School in Sault Sainte Marie. He played football because his high school did not have an official hockey team. Esposito was big and tall and played tight end and linebacker. These positions taught him how to be tough. That knowledge would serve him well in his future hockey career.

Esposito left St. Mary's halfway through his senior year to pursue his real passion—hockey. He tried out for the St. Catherine's TeePees, a junior A team in the Canadian Amateur League. The team was sponsored by the Chicago Black Hawks. Esposito, a center, was not good enough for the A team, and was sent to the B team in Sarnia, Ontario. The following year, after much hard work, Esposito was in a St. Catherine's uniform.

In 1963, twenty-one-year-old Esposito was promoted to the Black Hawks's team in the Eastern Hockey League. In his first season as a professional hockey player, Esposito scored 36 goals with 54 assists in just 71 games. Esposito followed that great season with an even better effort. He scored 26 goals with 54 assists in 43 games during the first half of the 1963-64 season. The Black Hawks noticed Esposito's scoring ability. They called him up to their NHL team in Chicago in January 1964. In his first NHL game, however, Esposito could not even get one shot on net. His first goal did not come until January 25.

Esposito scored only three goals in his first season with Chicago. But the Black Hawks were patient with him. Esposito worked well with the Hawks's superstar Bobby Hull. The Black Hawk manager decided to use Esposito as an assist man for their superstar. During the next three years, Esposito accepted his role as puck feeder to Hull.

In 1967, Esposito was traded to the Boston Bruins. The Bruins did not want Esposito to feed the puck to his teammates. They wanted him to score goals. Esposito was overjoyed. Now he could show the NHL what he really could do.

In his first season with the Bruins, Esposito scored 35 goals with a league-leading 49 assists. Esposito camped himself in front of the opponent's net where the opposing team's defensemen could not move him. Often, Esposito would score on rebounds. Other times, he would deflect shots into the net. The fans went wild for Esposito. Each time he scored they chanted, "Espo! Espo!"

In the 1968-69 season, Esposito tallied an incredible 126 points with 49 goals and a record 77 assists. Esposito was the first player to break the 100-point barrier. In 1970, he and Bobby Orr led the Bruins to a Stanley Cup Championship. During the play-offs, Esposito scored 13 goals with a total of 27 points. He had broken two more records. In the 1970-71 season, Esposito scored a record 76 goals in 78 games with 76 assists. His point total was an amazing 152, which was also a record.

*Esposito had his best year
with the Boston Bruins.*

*Here, with the N.Y. Rangers, Esposito continues
to be the goal scorer for the team.*

In the 1971-72 season, Esposito scored 66 goals with 67 assists, earning him the NHL scoring title for the third time in four years. He also helped to lead the Bruins to another Stanley Cup. Then in the 1972-73 season, Esposito scored 40 goals for the fifth straight season, setting yet another record.

After 1973, Esposito's statistics began to decline. He was eventually traded to the New York Rangers where he finished his playing career. Afterwards, Esposito traded his skates for a coaching position with the Rangers. Years later, he became their general manager.

A four-time All-Star, Esposito changed the face of hockey with his phenomenal scoring ability. He turned hockey from a slow, defensive game into a fast-paced scoring contest, setting the standards which today's stars aspire to.

The Golden Jet

Robert (Bobby) Hull was born January 3, 1939, in Point Anne, Ontario, Canada. His father was a farmer who had wanted to play professional hockey. Before Hull reached his third birthday, his father put him on skates for the first time. A year later, Hull had a sawed-off hockey stick in his hands. With it, he practiced puck handling and shooting. Already, Hull had his father's love for hockey. By the time he turned five years old, Hull was playing hockey with boys twice his age. He also played hockey with his younger brother, Dennis.

In 1960, Bobby Hull posed in his Chicago Black Hawks uniform.

Hull grew to be a strong and muscular hockey player. In high school, Hull played for the Chicago Black Hawks's Junior B team in the Ontario Hockey Association. In 1954, he led his team to a league championship. Afterwards, Hull played three years for the Hawks's Junior A team. After tearing up the league with his powerful skating and shooting, Hull was promoted to the Hawks's NHL team in Chicago in 1957. He was only eighteen years old.

In his first NHL season, Hull only scored 13 goals. But after the 1959-60 season, Hull had 39 goals with 81 total points. He was the best in the NHL. Suddenly, fans everywhere took notice of the rising Chicago star. People compared him to the great Gordie Howe of the Detroit Red Wings. Some thought he was better.

Hull was a fast skater. He could skate 29 miles per hour from one end of a rink to the other. No one, not even Howe, could skate that fast. Even more remarkable was Hull's terrifying slap shot, which he made famous. His shot was clocked at 118 miles per hour. Even his wrist shot broke the 100 mile per hour barrier.

*The combination of Hull's skating and shooting
speed won him the name "The Golden Jet."*

Combining his skating and shooting speed, Hull soon became a fearsome hockey player. The sportswriters began to call him "The Golden Jet." (Hull had blond hair.)

In the 1961-62 season, Hull scored 50 goals. He became the third man in NHL history to reach that lofty mark. With his 34 assists, Hull won his second scoring title. Then after the 1964-65 season, Hull was named the NHL's Most Valuable Player (MVP).

The following season, Hull broke the goal scoring record with 54 goals. For the second season in a row, Hull was named MVP. In 1966-67, Hull scored 52 goals. He followed that effort with 44 goals in 1967-68, making him the top goal scorer for three straight seasons. Then in 1968-69, Hull scored a remarkable 58 goals—a record at the time. Combined with 49 assists, Hull broke the 100-point barrier for the first time in his career. For his efforts, the Black Hawks made Hull the first $100,000-a-year hockey player.

In the 1961-62 season, Hull scored fifty goals.
He proudly holds the puck that was used
for the fiftieth goal.

OCT 25 '93   CHILI PUBLIC LIBRARY

Between 1969 and 1972, Hull scored 38, 44, and 50 goals each season. Hull was a hockey superstar and wanted to be paid like one. A new hockey league, the World Hockey Association (WHA), offered Hull a staggering $2.75 million. The WHA wanted Hull to become the player-coach for the Winnipeg Jets during the 1972-73 season. Hull accepted, making him the world's highest-paid athlete. After scoring 75 goals in 75 games for Winnipeg in one season, Hull retired in 1978. Now, he spends his time watching his son Brett play for the St. Louis Blues.

When he retired, Bobby Hull was second in career goals to Gordie Howe. His 1,153 points ranked him fourth. His 28 three-goal games (hat tricks) was first. No one has yet to play with as much power and speed as the Golden Jet, Bobby Hull.

Bobby Hull, a fierce competitor.

Gordie

Gordon (Gordie) Howe was born March 31,
1928, in Floral, Saskatchewan, Canada. Because
of the Great Depression, Howe's father had a
difficult time supporting his family of nine. The
Howes moved often as Mr. Howe searched for
work. Howe was a shy and quiet boy who did not
do well in school. He failed the third grade twice.
His formal education ended in the eighth grade.

*At seventeen, Gordy Howe signed with the
Detroit Red Wings. He remained with that team
throughout his twenty-five years in the NHL.*

Like most Canadian boys, Howe always found time to play hockey. His mother bought him his first pair of skates when he was six years old. By the time Howe was nine years old, he had already taken a keen interest in hockey. When he tried out for one of Saskatoon's teams in the midget hockey league, Howe was cut. He kept practicing and playing whenever he could. He finally found success at the King George School in Saskatoon, Saskatchewan. Because he was a slow and clumsy skater, Howe played goalie for two years. When he was eleven years old, Howe began to play right wing.

By the time he was fifteen years old, Howe was six feet tall and weighed two hundred pounds. He had powerful arms and broad shoulders. He was the strongest hockey player in Saskatoon. In 1944, sixteen-year-old Howe was spotted by the Detroit Red Wings. They signed him to a contract that included a $4,000 signing bonus.

Howe was sent to Detroit's Omaha team in the United States Hockey League. There, Howe scored 22 goals with 26 assists in 51 games. The following season, Howe was promoted to a Detroit Red Wing uniform. In his first game,

Howe scored a goal. He would remain with the Red Wings for his first twenty-five years in the NHL.

Howe remained a steady player throughout the 1940s. In 1950, Detroit made the Stanley Cup play-offs. Howe, already considered one of Detroit's stars, attempted to check (knock) an opponent into the boards. The opponent sidestepped the check, and Howe crashed headfirst into the boards. To save Howe's life, an operation had to be performed.

Howe was near death for days after the operation. Slowly, he made a complete recovery and was back with the Red Wings the next season. Instead of being hesitant on the ice, Howe's play turned fierce. Many opponents went out of their way to avoid him on the ice. In time, Howe was considered one of the strongest players in the NHL.

In 1953, Howe finished one of his greatest seasons. He scored 49 goals with 46 assists and won the scoring title. Throughout the remainder of the 1950s and into the 1960s, Howe won the scoring title five more times. He received the

Throughout the 1960s,
Howe won the MVP award six times.

Most Valuable Player award six times (a record). He also led the Red Wings to four Stanley Cup Championships.

The 1962-63 season was a particularly outstanding one for Howe. He won the scoring title and collected the MVP trophy. In 1965, Howe scored his 600th career goal. Though he was forty-one years old in the 1968-69 season, Howe remained a durable and steady player. That season was Howe's best. He scored 44 goals with 59 assists. After the 1970-71 season, Howe had 23 goals and 29 assists. Although he had played well, the season had been one of Howe's worst. Realizing this, Howe retired after twenty-five years in the NHL.

Almost immediately, Howe was named vice president of the Red Wings. In 1973, Howe was lured out of retirement by the WHA's Houston Aeros, who had already signed Howe's sons Marty and Mark. Howe played hockey with Houston for four years for $1 million. Afterwards, Howe signed with the New England Whalers and played two years with them. In 1979, the Whalers became part of the NHL and were renamed the Hartford Whalers. Howe was back in the NHL for his record 26th season. He played every game. In 1980, Howe retired for good.

Gordie Howe's accomplishments still shine brightly. In 17 of his 25 seasons with Detroit, Howe played in every Red Wing game. He was named to the All-Star team twenty-one times. Howe scored 67 play-off goals with 91 assists— 11 of which were game winners. When he retired from Hartford, he was Number One in the NHL in regular season games (1,767), goals (801), assists (1,049), and points (1,850).

Seems like old times ... Bobby Orr (left) and Gordie Howe still play the game as alumni of the Boston Bruins for charity and fund raisers.

The Great Gretzky

Wayne Gretzky was born January 26, 1961, in Brantford, Ontario, Canada. Gretzky grew up in a comfortable home. His father, Walter, worked for the Bell Telephone Company.

Gretzky was only two years old when he first learned to skate. Almost immediately, hockey became an obsession. As a young boy, Gretzky never played with toys. His only interest was hockey. He spent hours each day practicing his skills. In the winter when the ground froze in his

Wayne Gretzky

backyard, Gretzky would mow the grass short and bring out the lawn sprinkler to form an ice rink. Gretzky would practice skating with a puck around pylons he set up on the ice. In the summer when his friends played baseball, Gretzky would take a tennis ball and shoot it at the brick walls of his house. Gretzky did this every year for many years.

When he was five years old, Gretzky played on his first team: the Nadfrosky Steelers of the novice league. Most of the other boys in the league were nine and ten years old. Gretzky scored one goal that 1967-68 season.

The next season, Gretzky, a center, scored 27 goals. The season after that, Gretzky scored 104. Then, in 1970-71, Gretzky scored 196 goals.

By far, his biggest novice season came in 1971-72. That season, Gretzky scored 378 goals. In one tournament, Gretzky scored 50 goals in six games. Every time he got the puck, he scored. Every time. During another tournament game, Gretzky's team was down 5-0 in the third period. Gretzky went out and scored six straight goals.

*Wayne Gretzky of the Edmonton Oilers
skates around his opponent.*

His team won 6-5. In 1974, Gretzky scored his 1,000th minor hockey goal. By the time he was ten years old, a television network and *Sports Illustrated* magazine were reporting his accomplishments.

In 1975, Gretzky joined the Toronto Young Nationals in the Junior B hockey league. In his first game, he scored two goals. In the play-offs, Gretzky scored 73 points in 23 games. The Gretzky Era was about to begin.

Two years later, Gretzky was promoted to the Sault Sainte Marie Greyhounds of the Junior A league. Gretzky wanted number 9 on his jersey (his hero, Gordie Howe of the Detroit Red Wings, wore the same number). A teammate already had the number and would not give it up. Gretzky settled for 99—a number he would retain throughout his hockey career.

People had their doubts about Gretzky. He was not very big or very fast. Besides, he was only sixteen years old. But Gretzky was an outstanding playmaker. He could pass and shoot with pinpoint accuracy. In his first game, Gretzky had three goals and three assists and was named player of the game. The critics fell silent. Gretzky went on to score 70 goals with 112 assists for the season, a new rookie record. Gretzky was named Rookie of the Year.

In 1978, Gretzky turned professional. He signed a contract with the Indianapolis Racers of the World Hockey Association (WHA) for an incredible $1.75 million for seven years. Gretzky scored three goals with three assists in his eight games in Indianapolis. Then the owner was forced to trade Gretzky because of financial difficulties.

Gretzky's new team was the Edmonton Oilers of the WHA. The Oilers were once the Houston Aeros—and one of their players was Gordie Howe. Now Gretzky would play hockey with his hero. Gretzky finished the season scoring 43 goals with 61 assists and was named Rookie of the Year. The following season, the Edmonton Oilers were accepted into the NHL. Would Wayne Gretzky continue to be a star?

Gretzky finished his first NHL season with 51 goals and 83 assists, tying for the scoring crown. In one game during the season, Gretzky had 7 assists—a new record. At nineteen years of age,

Gretzky became the youngest player ever to win the MVP award.

In the 1980-81 season, Gretzky got even better. In one game, he scored five goals and had two assists. Then late in the season, Gretzky broke Phil Esposito's most-points-in-one-season record. Later, he broke Bobby Orr's most-assists-in-one-season record. Gretzky finished the season with 55 goals and 109 assists for 164 points. Gretzky had become the youngest player ever to win the scoring title. In the play-offs, Gretzky had 5 assists in one game and finished with 7 goals and 14 assists in 9 games total. For his efforts during the season, Gretzky earned the MVP award for the second year in a row.

The 1980-81 season was incredible—impossible to top, the critics said. Not even the "Great Gretzky," as the press was calling the Edmonton superstar, could hope to surpass those numbers. But the greatest season for Gretzky was still to come.

The "Great Gretzky"

*Gretzky holds up the Stanley Cup after the
Edmonton Oilers won the championship.*

The next season, Gretzky became the best ever. In late December 1981, Gretzky scored 9 goals in 2 games to give him a total of 50 goals in just 39 games—another NHL record. He finished the season with an incredible 92 goals and 120 assists for 212 points—all of which were records for scoring in one season. For the third season in a row, Gretzky won the MVP award. For the second season in a row, he earned the scoring title. Then the twenty-one-year-old superstar signed a twenty-one year contract worth $20 million dollars. But despite all his greatness, Gretzky and Edmonton had yet to win a Stanley Cup championship.

In 1984, Gretzky and the Oilers ended the New York Islanders's four-year domination of the play-offs by winning their first Stanley Cup. The following season, Gretzky led the Oilers to another Stanley Cup Championship, as Gretzky set a record for most points in one play-off season with 47. By 1985, Gretzky had won his sixth straight MVP award.

*The Great Gretzky was traded
to the L.A. Kings in August of 1988.*

Gretzky and the Oilers did not return to the Stanley Cup finals until 1987, when they won again. Afterwards, the twenty-six-year-old Gretzky received his eighth straight MVP award. In 1988, Gretzky reached another milestone when he broke Gordie Howe's career assist record of 1,049. It had taken Gretzky nine years to do what Howe had done in twenty-six. Gretzky finished the season by leading the Oilers to their fourth Stanley Cup championship in five years.

In August 1988, Gretzky was involved in one of the most shocking sports events of the decade. The oilers announced they had traded their superstar to the Los Angeles Kings. Later in the season, Gretzky made history one more time when he broke Howe's career points record. Gretzky did it in Edmonton, against the Oilers.

How long will Wayne Gretzky play? How many more records will he establish? It is hard to say—just as hard as finding a hockey player who will become greater than the Great Gretzky.

Gretzky faces off against the Toronto Maple Leafs